MASTERING SOCIAL MEDIA MANAGEMENT WITH AI

Temitope Aluko

CONTENTS

INTRODUCTION

Harnessing the Power of AI: Unleash
Your Social Media Potential

Welcome to the digital era, where social media has become an integral part of our personal and professional lives. In this fast-paced digital landscape, effective social media management is the key to capturing the attention of your audience and standing out from the competition.

However, with millions of users and countless posts flooding social media platforms every second, how can you ensure that your content shines through and resonates with your target audience? This is where the power of Artificial Intelligence (AI) comes into play.

In this practical handbook, "Mastering Social Media Management with AI," we will delve into the world of AI and its transformative impact on content creation and management. Whether you are a social media enthusiast, a seasoned marketer, or a business owner looking to elevate your online presence, this book will equip you with the knowledge and tools to navigate the ever-evolving landscape of social media using cutting-edge AI technologies.

Discover the Rise of AI in Social Media Management as we explore the incredible ways in which AI is revolutionizing the industry. From intelligent content generation to automated scheduling and data-driven insights, you'll unlock a treasure trove of possibilities that will supercharge your social media strategy.

But the benefits of AI go far beyond efficiency and convenience. Learn how AI can enhance your Content Creation and Management process, helping you craft engaging headlines, captions, and visuals that captivate your audience. Uncover the secrets of successful automation, enabling you to schedule and post content effortlessly, ensuring your brand remains consistently active and relevant.

Prepare to analyze and optimize your performance as we dive into AI-driven analytics. Discover the power of tracking key metrics, interpreting data, and implementing data-driven decisions that yield tangible results. We'll guide you through the process of monitoring customer engagement, managing support queries with AI chatbots, and leveraging influencer marketing to maximize your reach and impact.

Ethics and responsible AI usage are also at the forefront of this handbook. We will explore the importance of privacy, data protection, and addressing bias in AI algorithms, ensuring you wield the power of AI responsibly and ethically.

Finally, peer into the future as we discuss emerging trends and technologies that will shape the landscape of social media management. Stay ahead of the curve by embracing AI-powered trend analysis, anticipating industry shifts, and incorporating innovative approaches to captivate your audience.

This comprehensive guide is your passport to unlocking the full potential of social media management with AI. Get ready to embark on a journey that will transform your social media presence and elevate your brand to new heights. Let's dive in and discover how to master social media management with AI in this practical handbook for content creation.

CHAPTER 1

Understanding Social Media Platforms

In today's digital landscape, social media platforms have become essential for businesses and individuals alike to connect, engage, and grow their online presence. However, with the multitude of platforms available, it can be overwhelming to navigate and effectively leverage each one to its full potential.

In this chapter, we will take a deep dive into popular social media platforms, providing you with an in-depth understanding of their unique features and target audiences. Whether you're a seasoned social media manager or just starting out, this comprehensive guide will equip you with the knowledge and strategies you need to maximize the power of AI tools on each platform.

Discover how to captivate your audience on Facebook, Instagram, Twitter, LinkedIn, and more by tailoring your content creation approach to their specific preferences and behaviors. Unleash the true potential of AI as we explore the cutting-edge tools and techniques that will revolutionize your social media management game.

From crafting compelling headlines to designing eye-catching visuals, you'll learn how to create engaging content that grabs attention and drives results. Dive into the world of automated scheduling and posting and witness firsthand how AI can streamline your workflow and boost your productivity. By harnessing the power of AI analytics tools, you'll gain valuable insights into your performance metrics, enabling you to make data-driven decisions and continually optimize your social media strategy.

But that's not all. We'll also delve into customer engagement and support, exploring how AI-powered chatbots and sentiment analysis can enhance your interactions with your audience. Discover the secrets to successful influencer marketing campaigns, as we guide you through the process of finding, collaborating with, and measuring the impact of influencers on your brand.

Stay ahead of the curve with our insights on emerging trends and technologies in social media management, and explore the ethical considerations surrounding AI usage in the digital realm. Gain the knowledge and skills you need to navigate the ever-changing landscape of social media and future-proof your strategy.

Are you ready to unlock the power of social media and revolutionize your content creation process with AI? Join us on this transformative journey as we equip you with the tools and strategies to master social media management. It's time to make your mark and take your brand to new heights. Get ready to become a social media powerhouse.

Overview Of Popular Social Media Platforms

In today's digital landscape, social media platforms have become an integral part of our lives. They provide a space for individuals and businesses to connect, share, and engage with a global audience. To effectively manage social media presence, it's crucial to understand the popular platforms and their unique features. This chapter will provide an overview of the most widely used social media platforms and offer insights into their key features and target audiences.

Facebook: The All-in-One Social Networking Giant

Facebook is the largest social media platform with billions of users worldwide. It offers a diverse range of features, including personal profiles, business pages, groups, events, and a robust advertising platform. With a predominantly adult user base, Facebook is an ideal platform for building brand awareness, driving traffic, and engaging with a broad audience.

Instagram: Visual Storytelling and Influencer Culture

Instagram is a visual-centric platform that focuses on photo and video sharing. It has gained immense popularity, particularly among younger demographics. With features like Stories, Reels, and IGTV, Instagram provides a creative space for businesses to showcase their products and services. Influencer marketing is a prominent aspect of Instagram, making it an excellent platform for brand collaborations and reaching niche audiences.

Twitter: Real-Time News and Conversations

Twitter is known for its fast-paced and concise nature, where users share thoughts, news updates, and engage in conversations through tweets. With its character limit, Twitter encourages brevity and real-time interactions. It is widely used for customer support, thought leadership, and staying updated on current trends. Hashtags play a significant role in amplifying content and joining relevant conversations on Twitter.

LinkedIn: Professional Networking and B2B Connections

LinkedIn is the go-to platform for professional networking and B2B interactions. It caters to a primarily professional audience and offers features such as personal and company profiles, job postings, industry groups, and content sharing. LinkedIn is valuable for building professional relationships, establishing thought leadership, and generating leads in the business-to-business (B2B) space.

YouTube: Video Content and Entertainment Hub

YouTube is the world's largest video-sharing platform, offering a vast collection of user-generated and professional content. It is a powerhouse for video marketing, educational content, tutorials, and entertainment. With the potential to reach a massive audience, businesses can leverage YouTube to engage viewers through compelling visual storytelling.

Key Features And Target Audiences

To master social media management, it is essential to grasp the key features and understand the target audiences of different platforms. This chapter will provide an overview of the most popular social media platforms and delve into their unique features and the specific demographics they cater to.

Facebook: The All-in-One Social Networking Giant

Key Features: Personal Profiles: Facebook allows individuals to create personal profiles, connect with friends, and share updates, photos, and videos.

Business Pages: Businesses can create dedicated pages to promote their products, services, and engage with their target audience.

Groups: Facebook groups provide a space for like-minded individuals to connect, discuss topics of interest, and foster communities.

Events: Users can create and promote events, inviting others to attend and share details with their networks.

Advertising Platform: Facebook offers a robust advertising platform for businesses to reach their target audience with precision.

Target Audiences: Facebook has a broad user base, encompassing individuals of various age groups and demographics.

It is particularly popular among adults, making it an ideal platform for businesses targeting this segment.

Facebook's advertising capabilities allow businesses to define specific demographics, interests, and behaviors to reach their desired audience effectively.

Instagram: Visual Storytelling and Influencer Culture

Key Features: Photo and Video Sharing: Instagram primarily focuses on visual content, allowing users to share photos and videos.

Stories: Instagram Stories offer a temporary and immersive way to share content, often used to provide behind-the-scenes glimpses, product teasers, or engaging narratives.

Reels: This feature enables users to create and share short, creative videos, similar to TikTok.

IGTV: Instagram TV allows users to post longer videos, making it suitable for tutorials, product demonstrations, or vlogs.

Influencer Culture: Instagram is known for its influencer marketing culture, with individuals and brands collaborating to reach niche audiences.

Target Audiences: Instagram has a predominantly younger user base, appealing to millennials and Gen Z.

It attracts individuals interested in visual content, lifestyle inspiration, fashion, travel, and creative expression.

Brands looking to engage with younger audiences or those with visually appealing products can find great success on Instagram.

Twitter: Real-Time News and Conversations

Key Features: Tweets: Twitter's main feature is the ability to share short messages called tweets, limited to a specific character count.

Hashtags: Twitter utilizes hashtags to categorize and connect conversations around specific topics, allowing users to follow and participate in discussions.

Retweets and Likes: Users can retweet others' tweets to share them with their followers or express approval by liking them.

Replies and Mentions: Twitter encourages conversations through replies to tweets and mentions of other users in tweets.

Target Audiences: Twitter attracts a diverse user base, including individuals, brands, journalists, and thought leaders.

It appeals to those seeking real-time news updates, engaging in conversations around trending topics, and expressing opinions.

Businesses looking for timely interactions, customer support, or engagement with industry influencers often find value on Twitter.

LinkedIn: Professional Networking and B2B Connections

Key Features:Professional Profiles: LinkedIn allows individuals to create professional profiles, showcasing their work experience, skills, and achievements.

Company Pages: Businesses can create company pages to establish a professional presence, share company news, and engage with their professional network.

Groups: LinkedIn groups provide a platform for professionals to connect, discuss industry-specific topics, and exchange insights.

Job Postings: Companies can post job openings and connect with potential candidates through LinkedIn's job board.

Target Audiences: LinkedIn caters to professionals across various industries and is widely used for networking, recruitment, and B2B interactions.

It appeals to individuals seeking career development opportunities, industry insights, and professional connections.

Businesses targeting professionals, offering B2B products or services, or looking to establish thought leadership often find LinkedIn to be a valuable platform.

YouTube: Video Content and Entertainment Hub

Key Features: Video Sharing: YouTube is a video-centric platform, allowing users to upload, share, and watch videos.

Channels: Users can create dedicated channels to curate and showcase their video content.

Subscriptions: Users can subscribe to channels they are interested in, receiving updates and notifications when new videos are uploaded.

Monetization: YouTube provides opportunities for content creators to monetize their videos through advertising, sponsorships, and memberships.

Target Audiences: YouTube appeals to a wide range of users, from individuals seeking entertainment and educational content to businesses promoting their products or services.

It attracts audiences interested in video content, tutorials, music, gaming, and various forms of entertainment.

Businesses looking to engage with audiences through video marketing or educational content can leverage YouTube's extensive reach.

Understanding the key features and target audiences of social media platforms is crucial for effective content creation, engagement, and audience targeting. By aligning your social media strategies with the unique characteristics of each platform, you can maximize your reach, engage with the right audience, and achieve your social media management goals.

Maximizing AI Tools For Each Platform

To optimize social media management, leveraging AI tools specific to each platform can significantly enhance efficiency and effectiveness. Here are some ways AI can be utilized on popular social media platforms:

Content Creation: AI-powered tools can generate content ideas, provide writing suggestions, and create engaging visuals. These tools utilize machine learning algorithms to analyze trends and user preferences, assisting in the creation of compelling and tailored content for each platform.

Scheduling and Automation: AI-based social media management tools allow users to schedule posts, automate repetitive tasks, and optimize posting times based on audience engagement patterns. This streamlines content distribution and ensures consistent and timely delivery across multiple platforms.

Sentiment Analysis: AI algorithms can analyze user sentiments and engagement patterns, providing valuable insights into the performance of social media content. By understanding audience reactions, businesses can tailor their strategies and respond to feedback effectively.

Ad Targeting and Optimization: AI-powered advertising platforms on social media enable precise targeting based on demographics, interests, and behavior. These tools can automatically optimize ad campaigns, maximizing return on investment (ROI) and reaching the desired target audience.

In conclusion, understanding the popular social media platforms and their unique features is crucial for effective social media management. By harnessing AI tools tailored to each platform, businesses can streamline content creation, scheduling, and optimization processes. The next chapter will delve deeper into crafting engaging content with AI, further enhancing your social media management skills.

CHAPTER 2

Crafting Engaging Content with AI

Leveraging AI For Content Ideation And Brainstorming

In today's fast-paced digital landscape, content creation plays a pivotal role in successful social media management. However, consistently generating fresh and engaging ideas can be a challenging task. This is where the power of AI comes into play. Artificial intelligence algorithms can analyze vast amounts of data, identify patterns, and provide valuable insights to fuel your content ideation and brainstorming process.

When leveraging AI for content ideation, there are several techniques and tools you can use to spark creativity and generate compelling ideas. Let's explore some of them:

Trend Analysis: AI-powered tools can monitor social media platforms, news articles, and industry trends to identify popular topics and discussions. By staying up-to-date with the latest trends, you can create content that resonates with your target audience and capitalizes on current interests.

Keyword Research: AI-based keyword research tools can help you identify the most relevant and high-performing keywords related to your niche. These tools provide insights into search volume, competition, and related keywords, enabling you to optimize your content for better visibility and engagement.

Natural Language Generation (NLG): NLG is a branch of AI that focuses on generating human-like text. With NLG tools, you can input data or parameters, and the AI algorithm will generate coherent and contextually appropriate content. This can be especially useful for creating product descriptions, blog articles, and social media posts.

Content Discovery Platforms: AI-driven content discovery platforms can provide personalized recommendations based on your interests and preferences. These platforms analyze your browsing behavior, social media activity, and content consumption patterns to suggest relevant articles, videos, and infographics that can inspire your content creation.

Writing Captivating Headlines And Captions

Once you have generated a pool of ideas, the next step is to craft captivating headlines and captions that grab your audience's attention and entice them to engage with your content. AI can assist you in this process by offering insights and suggestions to optimize your headlines and captions for maximum impact.

Sentiment Analysis: AI algorithms can analyze the sentiment behind your content and provide feedback on the emotional tone of your headlines and captions. This can help you strike the right balance and tailor your messaging to resonate with your audience.

A/B Testing: AI-powered A/B testing tools allow you to test different headline and caption variations to determine which ones perform better. By experimenting with different phrasing, wording, or formatting, you can identify the most effective approach to engage your audience.

Language Enhancement: AI tools equipped with natural language processing capabilities can offer suggestions to improve the clarity, readability, and overall quality of your headlines and captions. These tools can help you eliminate grammar errors, enhance vocabulary usage, and ensure your messaging is concise and impactful.

Designing Eye-Catching Visuals With AI

Visual content plays a crucial role in capturing the attention of social media users. Incorporating AI into your visual content creation process can significantly enhance the appeal and effectiveness of your visuals.

Image Recognition and Tagging: AI-powered image recognition tools can analyze the content of an image and automatically generate descriptive tags or labels. This simplifies the process of organizing and categorizing your visual assets, making them easily searchable and accessible for future use.

Image Editing and Enhancement: AI-driven image editing tools can automatically enhance and optimize your visuals by adjusting brightness, contrast, colors, and other parameters. These tools can also remove background elements or apply filters to create visually appealing images that align with your brand aesthetics.

Automated Design Tools: AI-powered design tools offer pre-designed templates and layouts that can be customized to create professional-looking graphics, infographics, and social media posts. These tools often come with built-in AI algorithms that assist in suggesting design elements, color schemes, and font combinations that are visually pleasing and engaging.

By incorporating AI into your content creation process, you can unlock a wealth of possibilities for crafting engaging and impactful content. Whether it's generating fresh ideas, optimizing headlines and captions, or designing eye-catching visuals, AI empowers you to take your social media management to new heights.

Remember, AI is a tool that should complement and enhance your creative abilities. Utilize its power while infusing your unique brand voice and style to create content that truly resonates with your audience.

CHAPTER 3

Automating Content Scheduling and Posting

I n today's fast-paced digital landscape, social media management has become increasingly complex. Fortunately, advancements in artificial intelligence (AI) have revolutionized the way businesses and individuals manage their social media presence. AI-powered social media management tools offer a wide range of capabilities that simplify and enhance various aspects of content creation, scheduling, posting, and analytics.

AI in social media management refers to the integration of machine learning algorithms and natural language processing techniques into software platforms specifically designed to assist in social media-related tasks. These tools leverage AI to automate and streamline processes, saving valuable time and resources while improving overall efficiency.

When it comes to choosing the right AI-powered social media management tool, it's essential to consider factors such as features, user interface, pricing, and customer support. To help you navigate through the vast array of options available, let's explore some popular AI-powered social media management tools.

Features And Benefits Of AI-Powered Tools

AI-powered social media management tools offer a plethora of features and functionalities that can significantly enhance your content scheduling and posting workflows. Let's explore some key features and how AI streamlines these processes:

Content Creation Assistance:

AI-powered tools provide intelligent content creation assistance by suggesting relevant topics, generating engaging captions, and even offering image recommendations. By leveraging natural language processing and image recognition algorithms, these tools save time and boost creativity by automating repetitive tasks and providing inspiration for compelling content.

Automated Scheduling and Posting:

AI streamlines the scheduling and posting of your content across multiple social media platforms. These tools analyze data patterns, user behavior, and engagement metrics to determine the optimal times for posting. By automating these processes, you can ensure consistent content delivery and maximize visibility without manual intervention.

Personalization and Audience Targeting:

AI-powered tools leverage machine learning algorithms to analyze audience data and create personalized content experiences. These tools can segment your audience based on demographics, interests, and behavior, allowing you to tailor your content for specific target groups. By delivering personalized content, you can increase engagement, build stronger relationships with your audience, and drive conversions.

Performance Analytics and Insights:

AI analytics capabilities provide detailed performance metrics and insights to evaluate the success of your social media campaigns. These tools track key metrics such as reach, engagement, click-through rates, and conversions. AI algorithms analyze this data to identify trends, patterns, and areas for improvement. By leveraging these insights, you can make data-driven decisions, refine your strategies, and optimize your content to achieve better results.

Sentiment Analysis and Brand Monitoring:

AI-powered tools can perform sentiment analysis, allowing you to gauge the sentiment associated with your brand and content. By analyzing user comments, mentions, and reviews, AI algorithms identify positive, negative, or neutral sentiments. This functionality enables you to monitor your brand's reputation, respond promptly to customer feedback, and mitigate potential crises.

Social Listening and Trend Identification:

AI-powered tools monitor social media conversations and identify trends and topics relevant to your industry or niche. By leveraging natural language processing and machine learning, these tools can sift through vast amounts of social media data to identify emerging trends, popular hashtags, and topics that resonate with your target audience. This feature helps you stay ahead of the curve, create timely content, and engage with trending discussions.

Workflow Automation and Collaboration:

AI-powered tools streamline workflow processes by automating repetitive tasks, facilitating collaboration, and ensuring smooth content management. These tools often provide features like content calendars, approval workflows, and collaboration platforms, allowing teams to coordinate their efforts efficiently. AI can also assist in content curation by suggesting relevant articles, news, and user-generated content.

The benefits of using AI-powered tools for content scheduling and posting are manifold. They save time by automating manual processes, increase efficiency by providing intelligent recommendations, optimize content delivery by analyzing data and user behavior, and empower you to make data-driven decisions for improved results. By harnessing AI capabilities, you can streamline your social media management, enhance engagement, and achieve your business objectives effectively.

Using AI-Powered Social Media Management Tools

In today's fast-paced digital world, managing social media accounts manually can be time-consuming and overwhelming. Fortunately, advancements in artificial intelligence (AI) have revolutionized social media management, providing efficient and effective solutions for content scheduling and posting. In this chapter, we will explore the power of AI-powered social media management tools and how they can streamline your content creation process.

Understanding the Role of AI in Content Scheduling and Posting

Artificial Intelligence (AI) has revolutionized the way businesses approach social media management. When it comes to content scheduling and posting, AI plays a pivotal role in automating repetitive tasks, optimizing performance, and enhancing overall efficiency. By leveraging AI in content management, social media managers can focus more on strategy, creativity, and engaging with their audience.

AI-driven algorithms analyze vast amounts of data, including user behavior, preferences, and historical performance metrics. This data analysis enables AI-powered social media management tools to make data-backed decisions regarding the best times to post, content types to prioritize, and the frequency of posting. Through this data-driven approach, AI empowers businesses to improve their content strategies and maximize engagement, ultimately leading to increased brand visibility and conversion rates.

Exploring Popular AI-Powered Social Media Management Platforms

In recent years, numerous AI-powered social media management platforms have emerged, each offering unique features and functionalities. Some of the popular platforms include:

Social Media Content Schedulers: These tools allow you to plan, create, and schedule your social media posts in advance. They often integrate with multiple social media platforms, offering a centralized dashboard for content management.

AI-Driven Content Curation Tools: These platforms use AI algorithms to curate relevant and trending content from various sources, making it easier for social media managers to discover engaging content for their audience.

Sentiment Analysis Tools: These tools use AI to analyze the sentiment behind social media interactions and comments, helping brands gauge audience reactions to their content and adjust their strategies accordingly.

Automated Social Media Advertising Platforms: AI-powered ad platforms optimize ad targeting, budget allocation, and bidding strategies, ensuring that your social media advertising efforts yield maximum returns on investment (ROI).

Features And Functionalities Of AI-Driven Tools

AI-powered social media management tools come equipped with a range of powerful features and functionalities that streamline the content creation and posting process. Some common features include:

Automated Scheduling: The ability to schedule social media posts in advance based on optimal posting times determined by AI algorithms.

Content Recommendations: AI-generated content suggestions based on audience preferences and trending topics.

Performance Analytics: In-depth data analysis, offering insights into post reach, engagement, and conversion rates, enabling data-driven decision-making.

Social Listening: Monitoring social media platforms for mentions, brand sentiment, and industry trends.

Automated Responses: AI chatbots that can engage with users, answer common questions, and provide customer support on social media.

Selecting The Right Tool For Your Social Media Objectives

With a plethora of AI-powered social media management tools available, choosing the right one for your specific objectives is crucial. Consider the following factors when making your selection:

Scope of Integration: Ensure that the tool integrates with the social media platforms you use to manage your brand presence effectively.

Customizability: Look for platforms that allow customization to align with your brand's unique tone, style, and content requirements.

Performance Analytics: Prioritize tools that provide robust analytics and insights to measure the success of your social media campaigns.

Budget and Scalability: Evaluate the cost of the tool and whether it aligns with your budget. Additionally, consider whether the tool can scale with your growing social media needs.

User-Friendliness: Opt for a tool that is intuitive and user-friendly, allowing your team to quickly adapt and make the most of its features.

By carefully assessing your requirements and comparing the features of different AI-powered social media management tools, you can find the perfect fit that aligns with your social media objectives and maximizes your content scheduling and posting efficiency.

Optimizing Posting Times And Frequency

To maximize the impact of your social media content, it's essential to optimize posting times and frequency. AI-powered social media management tools can help you determine the best times to post, ensure consistent engagement, and reach your target audience effectively. This section explores various strategies that leverage AI analytics to optimize your content scheduling and posting practices.

Analyzing Peak Engagement Periods with AI Analytics

AI analytics tools offer valuable insights into your audience's behavior and engagement patterns on different social media platforms. By analyzing historical data and user interactions, these tools can identify peak engagement periods when your audience is most active. Understanding these patterns allows you to strategically schedule your posts during times when your content is likely to receive maximum visibility and interaction.

Identifying Ideal Posting Times for Different Time Zones

If your target audience spans multiple time zones, it's crucial to post at times that cater to each region's peak activity. AI-powered tools can analyze audience demographics and engagement data across various time zones to identify the best posting times for each location. This approach ensures that your content reaches different segments of your audience at the most opportune moments, increasing the chances of higher engagement.

Tailoring Content Schedules to Target Audience Behavior

AI-driven social media management tools can also help you understand your audience's behavior and preferences on different days of the week and even during specific seasons or events. By recognizing content consumption patterns, you can tailor your content schedules to align with your audience's preferences. For example, if your audience tends to be more active on weekends, you can adjust your posting frequency and timing accordingly.

Implementing AI-Generated Content Queues For Consistent Posting

Consistency is key to maintaining engagement and building a loyal audience. AI-powered social media tools can generate content queues, allowing you to plan and schedule posts in advance. These tools consider your optimized posting times and frequency to create a steady stream of content, even during periods when manual posting may be challenging. By implementing content queues, you ensure a consistent presence on social media, keeping your audience engaged and informed.

Moreover, AI-generated content queues can help you strike a balance between promotional and informative content, making your social media strategy more versatile and engaging. By utilizing a mix of content types and formats, you can better connect with your audience and cater to their varying interests.

Optimizing posting times and frequency is a crucial aspect of successful social media management. Leveraging AI analytics enables you to make data-driven decisions and refine your content scheduling strategy for maximum impact. By identifying peak engagement periods, accommodating different time zones, understanding audience behavior, and implementing content queues, you can maintain a consistent and engaging social media presence that resonates with your target audience. As you continue to use AI-powered tools, be open to analyzing performance metrics and making adjustments to your content strategy to stay ahead in the dynamic world of social media.

Implementing Evergreen Content Strategies

Evergreen content is a timeless and valuable asset for any social media strategy. It remains relevant to your audience over an extended period, offering long-term benefits in terms of engagement, traffic, and conversions. AI-powered tools can significantly enhance your evergreen content strategy by assisting in content repurposing, ensuring relevance, and measuring its long-term impact. Let's explore how to effectively implement evergreen content strategies with the help of AI.

Understanding the Concept of Evergreen Content

Evergreen content refers to pieces of content that retain their relevance and value to your audience regardless of the passage of time. Unlike topical or time-sensitive content, evergreen content remains useful and informative even months or years after its publication. This can include comprehensive how-to guides, tutorials, educational resources, and expert insights that address common pain points or questions within your niche.

Leveraging AI for Repurposing and Refreshing Evergreen Content

AI can be an invaluable tool for breathing new life into existing evergreen content. By leveraging natural language processing (NLP) capabilities, AI can analyze your content and identify opportunities for repurposing. For instance, it can suggest converting a blog post into an infographic, transforming a tutorial into a video, or creating a podcast episode from an in-depth article.

Additionally, AI can help you identify outdated information within your evergreen content and suggest updates to keep it accurate and valuable. By periodically refreshing your evergreen content based on AI recommendations, you can maintain its relevance and authority, enticing your audience to return for valuable insights.

Techniques to Keep Evergreen Content Timeless and Relevant

Creating evergreen content requires a careful approach to ensure that it remains timeless and relevant. AI can aid in identifying evergreen topics that have enduring popularity or consistently generate interest among your target audience. By analyzing user behavior, search trends, and historical data, AI tools can help you generate content ideas with long-term appeal.

Furthermore, AI can assist in optimizing evergreen content for search engines, ensuring that it ranks well for relevant keywords and continues to attract organic traffic over time. By refining meta tags, headlines, and content structure, you can improve the discoverability and visibility of your evergreen pieces.

Measuring The Long-Term Impact Of Evergreen Content With AI Metrics

AI-powered analytics tools play a crucial role in evaluating the long-term impact of evergreen content. Standard metrics like page views and shares are important, but AI-driven tools can delve deeper into data analysis. By tracking user engagement, bounce rates, time on page, and conversion rates, AI metrics provide insights into how well your evergreen content resonates with your audience and drives meaningful interactions.

Furthermore, AI can help you understand how evergreen content contributes to your overall social media and marketing goals. By attributing conversions and customer journeys to specific evergreen pieces, AI metrics help you determine the true value and ROI of your evergreen content strategy.

Implementing evergreen content strategies with the assistance of AI can significantly enhance your social media presence and content marketing efforts. By understanding the concept of evergreen content, leveraging AI for repurposing and refreshing, ensuring timelessness and relevance, and measuring long-term impact with AI metrics, you can create a powerful content ecosystem that continuously engages and delights your audience. Embrace the capabilities of AI to craft a sustainable content strategy that delivers lasting value and fosters meaningful connections with your audience over time.

Balancing Automation And Personalization

Social media management requires a delicate balance between automation and personalization. While AI-powered automation can significantly streamline your workflow and boost efficiency, maintaining a human touch in your content is vital to building authentic connections with your audience. In this section, we'll explore how to strike the right balance, leveraging AI for personalized content recommendations while ensuring your social media posts remain genuine and engaging.

The Role of Human Touch in Social Media Content

Human connection lies at the heart of successful social media marketing. People want to engage with brands that feel approachable, relatable, and authentic. While automation can help with scheduling and posting, it's essential to remember that social media is fundamentally about fostering relationships. Responding to comments, engaging in conversations, and showing empathy are all elements that require a human touch to establish trust and loyalty with your audience.

Utilizing AI For Personalized Content Recommendations

AI excels at analyzing vast amounts of data, enabling it to understand individual preferences and behavior patterns. Leverage AI-powered tools to gain insights into your audience's interests, engagement history, and demographics. This information can then be used to recommend personalized content to different segments of your audience, ensuring that your social media posts are relevant and resonate with each user.

By tailoring your content recommendations based on AI insights, you demonstrate that you understand and value your audience's needs, leading to stronger relationships and increased engagement.

Avoiding Over-Automation and Maintaining Authenticity

While automation can be efficient, over-reliance on AI-driven posting may result in a robotic and impersonal social media presence. Avoid using a one-size-fits-all approach when it comes to content scheduling and posting. Instead, identify key moments where personalization and genuine human interaction are essential.

For example, during special events or in response to significant news, consider taking a more hands-on approach by crafting bespoke messages that show empathy and understanding. This human touch will demonstrate your brand's authenticity and responsiveness, resonating with your audience on a deeper level.

Strategies To Humanize Automated Social Media Posts

Humanizing your automated social media posts involves adding personality and warmth to your content. Here are some strategies to achieve this:

a. Use Conversational Language: Write in a friendly and conversational tone that feels approachable and engaging.

b. Incorporate User-Generated Content (UGC): Share content created by your followers and customers, showcasing real experiences with your brand.

c. Be Transparent: If you're using chatbots or AI-driven responses, let your audience know upfront that they are interacting with automated systems. Honesty fosters trust.

d. Engage in Real-Time Conversations: Monitor your social media platforms for mentions and direct messages, and respond promptly to customer inquiries or feedback.

e. Celebrate Milestones and Events: Acknowledge important moments for your brand and audience, and celebrate achievements together.

Finding the right balance between automation and personalization is the key to a successful social media strategy. By using AI for personalized content recommendations and leveraging automation for content scheduling, you can optimize your social media efforts while maintaining an authentic human touch. Remember that behind every interaction on social media is a real person, and catering to their needs and interests will forge meaningful connections that drive loyalty and brand advocacy. Stay mindful of the human element in your social media content, and your audience will appreciate the genuine and valuable experience you provide.

CHAPTER 4

Analyzing Performance and Driving Results

In this chapter, we delve into the world of data-driven decision-making and explore how AI analytics tools can empower you to optimize your social media management efforts. By harnessing the power of AI, you'll be equipped with the knowledge and insights needed to make informed choices that drive tangible results.

Tracking Key Metrics With AI Analytics Tools

Discover how AI analytics tools can help you navigate the vast ocean of social media data and extract valuable insights. Learn how to effectively monitor key metrics such as engagement rates, reach, conversions, and more. Uncover the hidden patterns and trends within your data to gain a deeper understanding of your audience's behavior and preferences.

In the ever-evolving landscape of social media, tracking key metrics is vital for effective and successful content management. Fortunately, the emergence of AI analytics tools has revolutionized the way we measure and evaluate social media performance. In this chapter, we delve into the world of tracking key metrics using AI analytics tools, equipping you with the knowledge and skills to harness the power of data-driven insights.

To begin, let's explore the importance of tracking key metrics. When managing social media accounts, it's crucial to have a clear understanding of how your content is resonating with your audience. Tracking key metrics allows you to assess the impact and reach of your posts, measure engagement levels, and identify areas for improvement. By leveraging AI analytics tools, you gain access to real-time data, enabling you to make informed decisions and refine your content strategy for optimal results.

One of the primary benefits of AI analytics tools is their ability to provide granular insights into various metrics. From tracking likes, comments, and shares to monitoring click-through rates and conversions, these tools offer a comprehensive view of your social media performance. With AI algorithms at work, you can uncover patterns and correlations in the data that might have otherwise gone unnoticed, helping you identify successful strategies and areas that need improvement.

AI analytics tools also excel in providing real-time data. Unlike traditional analytics tools, AI-powered solutions can process vast amounts of data quickly and efficiently, allowing you to monitor your performance in real-time. This capability enables you to respond promptly to trends, adapt your content strategy, and seize opportunities as they arise. Whether it's tracking the performance of a new campaign or monitoring the impact of a timely post, AI analytics tools provide the agility and responsiveness needed to stay ahead in the ever-changing social media landscape.

Moreover, AI analytics tools offer advanced segmentation and audience analysis features. These tools can segment your audience based on various factors, such as demographics, interests, or behaviors, providing you with valuable insights into who your audience is and how they engage with your content. Armed with this knowledge, you can tailor your content to better resonate with your target audience, resulting in increased engagement and stronger connections.

As you embark on the journey of tracking key metrics with AI analytics tools, it's crucial to define your goals and identify the metrics that align with your objectives. Different metrics hold varying degrees of importance depending on your specific goals, whether it's brand awareness, lead generation, or customer engagement. By focusing on the metrics that matter most to your social media strategy, you can derive meaningful insights and measure the success of your efforts effectively.

In conclusion, AI analytics tools have revolutionized the way we track key metrics in social media management. By harnessing the power of data-driven insights, you can gain a comprehensive understanding of your social media performance and make informed decisions to optimize your content strategy. With real-time data, advanced segmentation, and the ability to uncover hidden patterns, AI analytics tools are indispensable assets in the journey toward mastering social media management with AI.

Interpreting Data And Identifying Trends

Unleash the power of data interpretation and trend analysis to unlock valuable opportunities for growth. We'll guide you through the process of extracting meaningful insights from complex data sets. Learn to identify patterns, spot emerging trends, and stay one step ahead of the competition. Empowered with this knowledge, you'll be able to fine-tune your content strategy and make data-backed decisions.

Data is the lifeblood of effective social media management, but raw data alone is meaningless without proper interpretation. In this chapter, we delve into the art of interpreting data and identifying trends, equipping you with the skills to extract valuable insights from the vast amount of information available to you.

Interpreting data involves transforming raw numbers and figures into actionable insights that can guide your content strategy and decision-making process. By analyzing and understanding the patterns and trends within your data, you can unlock a wealth of information that can drive your social media success.

One of the key aspects of data interpretation is identifying meaningful metrics and KPIs (Key Performance Indicators) that align with your goals. Rather than getting overwhelmed by a deluge of data, it's crucial to focus on the metrics that matter most to your social media strategy. For example, if your objective is to increase brand awareness, metrics such as reach and impressions would be highly relevant. If lead generation is your goal, metrics like click-through rates and conversions would hold greater importance. By narrowing down your focus to the metrics that directly impact your objectives, you can streamline your analysis and gain meaningful insights.

AI analytics tools play a crucial role in data interpretation, as they can handle vast amounts of data and provide powerful analytical capabilities. These tools use AI algorithms to analyze and identify patterns and correlations within your data, uncovering insights that might not be immediately apparent. For instance, AI can identify the types of content that generate the highest engagement or the optimal posting times that yield the best results. By leveraging the power of AI in data interpretation, you can extract deeper insights and make data-driven decisions.

Identifying trends within your data is another essential aspect of data interpretation. Trends can provide valuable information about the effectiveness of your content strategy, audience preferences, and shifts in the social media landscape. By identifying emerging trends, you can adapt your strategy accordingly and stay ahead of the curve. AI analytics tools can help in detecting trends by analyzing historical data and comparing it with current performance. They can identify changes in engagement levels, content performance, or audience behavior, allowing you to adjust your approach and capitalize on emerging opportunities.

Visualization is a powerful tool for data interpretation, as it allows you to present complex data in a visually appealing and easily understandable format. Charts, graphs, and infographics can help you identify patterns, spot anomalies, and communicate insights effectively. AI analytics tools often offer built-in visualization capabilities, allowing you to create compelling visual representations of your data with ease.

In conclusion, interpreting data and identifying trends are essential skills for effective social media management. By analyzing and understanding your data, you can gain valuable insights that can guide your content strategy and decision-making process. With the aid of AI analytics tools, you can uncover hidden patterns, identify emerging trends, and make data-driven decisions to optimize your social media performance. By mastering the art of data interpretation, you'll be well-equipped to stay ahead of the curve and achieve your social media goals.

A/B Testing And Optimization Techniques

Discover the art of experimentation through A/B testing and optimization techniques. Learn how to create controlled experiments to compare different approaches and determine the most effective strategies for your social media campaigns. By implementing systematic testing and optimization, you'll be able to optimize your content, ads, and campaigns to achieve higher engagement, conversions, and overall success.

In the realm of social media management, staying ahead of the competition requires constant experimentation and refinement. A/B testing, combined with optimization techniques, is a powerful methodology that allows you to compare and improve different versions of your content, ensuring that you are delivering the most effective and impactful messages to your audience. In this chapter, we explore the art of A/B testing and delve into various optimization techniques, empowering you to elevate your social media strategy to new heights.

A/B testing involves creating two or more versions of a particular element, such as a post, advertisement, or landing page, and presenting them to different segments of your audience. By comparing the performance of these variations, you can identify which version resonates best with your audience and yields the desired outcomes. AI-driven A/B testing tools make this process even more efficient by automating the creation and analysis of these variations, saving you time and effort.

To begin, it is crucial to define clear objectives for your A/B tests. Whether you aim to increase engagement, improve click-through rates, or drive conversions, having specific goals in mind will guide your testing process and allow you to measure success effectively. By focusing on one objective at a time, you can obtain actionable insights and refine your strategy accordingly.

When conducting A/B tests, it is essential to isolate and test only one variable at a time. This ensures that the impact on performance can be attributed to the specific element being tested. For instance, if you are testing different post headlines, keep all other factors, such as the accompanying visuals or posting times, consistent across the variations. By isolating variables, you can accurately determine which element drives the desired outcome and make data-informed decisions.

Once you have collected sufficient data from your A/B tests, it's time to analyze and interpret the results. AI analytics tools can assist you in this process by providing statistical analysis and data visualization. You can uncover which version performed better based on key metrics such as engagement rates, click-through rates, or conversions. By understanding the data and identifying significant differences between variations, you can identify winning strategies and optimize your content accordingly.

Optimization techniques go hand in hand with A/B testing, as they enable you to continuously improve and refine your content based on the insights gained from the testing process. AI analytics tools can help identify patterns and trends in the data, enabling you to make data-driven optimizations. Whether it's adjusting the content format, refining the messaging, or optimizing the timing of your posts, these techniques allow you to enhance your social media strategy incrementally.

Iterative testing and optimization should be a continuous process. As you gain insights from each A/B test, apply the learnings to subsequent tests, gradually refining and optimizing your content strategy. This approach allows you to stay agile and adapt to changes in audience preferences, platform algorithms, and industry trends.

In conclusion, A/B testing and optimization techniques are essential tools for maximizing the effectiveness of your social media strategy. By conducting A/B tests and analyzing the results with AI analytics tools, you can identify winning strategies, isolate variables, and make data-informed decisions. Through iterative testing and continuous optimization, you can refine your content to deliver the most impactful messages to your audience, leading to improved engagement, conversions, and overall social media success. Embrace the power of A/B testing and optimization, and elevate your social media management to new levels of performance.

CHAPTER 5

Managing Customer Engagement and Support

Enhancing Customer Experience With AI Chatbots

In today's fast-paced digital world, providing exceptional customer experience has become paramount for businesses striving to stand out from the crowd. And when it comes to managing customer engagement and support, AI chatbots have emerged as invaluable tools. These intelligent virtual assistants are revolutionizing the way businesses interact with their customers, delivering personalized and prompt assistance round the clock.

In this chapter, we delve into the realm of AI-powered chatbots and explore how they can elevate your customer experience to new heights. Through the implementation of AI chatbots, you can engage with your customers in real-time, addressing their queries and concerns without delay. These chatbots are capable of analyzing customer requests, understanding intent, and providing relevant and accurate responses instantaneously.

In today's rapidly evolving digital landscape, businesses are constantly seeking innovative ways to enhance their customer experience. One powerful tool that has gained significant popularity is AI chatbots. These intelligent virtual assistants have revolutionized customer interactions, providing personalized and prompt assistance round the clock.

AI chatbots have the ability to engage with customers in real-time, catering to their needs and addressing their queries with efficiency and accuracy. By analyzing customer requests and understanding their intent, these chatbots can provide relevant and timely responses, ensuring a seamless and satisfying customer experience.

One of the key advantages of AI chatbots is their availability 24/7. Unlike human agents, chatbots are not bound by working hours or time zones. Customers can reach out to a chatbot at any time, receiving instant assistance without any delays. This round-the-clock availability not only enhances customer satisfaction but also boosts efficiency and productivity for businesses, as they can handle customer inquiries and support requests even outside of regular working hours.

Moreover, AI chatbots can handle multiple conversations simultaneously, providing a swift response to each customer without compromising quality. This multitasking capability allows businesses to scale their customer support operations without the need for additional human resources, saving both time and costs.

In addition to their responsiveness, AI chatbots can offer a personalized experience to each customer. Through machine learning algorithms, chatbots can learn from previous interactions, understanding individual preferences and tailoring their responses accordingly. This personalized touch makes customers feel valued and understood, leading to a stronger connection with the brand.

Furthermore, AI chatbots can assist customers with various tasks, such as providing product recommendations, guiding them through the purchase process, or offering troubleshooting assistance. By automating these routine tasks, businesses can free up human agents to focus on more complex and high-value interactions, further improving the overall customer experience.

However, it is important to note that while AI chatbots excel in handling routine and repetitive tasks, there are instances where human intervention is necessary. Recognizing these situations and seamlessly transitioning customers to human agents when needed is crucial to maintaining a positive customer experience.

To implement AI chatbots effectively, businesses should ensure a smooth integration with their existing customer support systems. This includes training the chatbots with relevant data, constantly monitoring their performance, and regularly updating their knowledge base to ensure accurate and up-to-date responses.

AI-Driven Sentiment Analysis And Reputation Management

In the age of social media and online reviews, monitoring your brand's reputation and understanding customer sentiment has become crucial. With the power of AI-driven sentiment analysis, you can gain valuable insights into how your customers perceive your brand and tailor your strategies accordingly.

In this section, we uncover the potential of AI-driven sentiment analysis and reputation management. By leveraging advanced algorithms, you can automatically analyze customer feedback, reviews, and social media conversations to gauge the sentiment behind them. This enables you to detect positive or negative sentiments associated with your brand, identify potential issues, and take proactive measures to maintain a positive reputation.

In today's digital age, where online reputation can make or break a business, understanding customer sentiment and managing reputation effectively has become vital. This is where AI-driven sentiment analysis comes into play. By harnessing the power of artificial intelligence, businesses can gain valuable insights into customer sentiment, enabling them to make data-driven decisions and take proactive measures to maintain a positive reputation.

AI-driven sentiment analysis involves the use of advanced algorithms to analyze large volumes of customer feedback, reviews, and social media conversations. These algorithms can identify and classify sentiments associated with specific products, services, or brands, providing businesses with a comprehensive understanding of customer perception.

One of the key advantages of AI-driven sentiment analysis is its ability to process vast amounts of data quickly and accurately. Human analysis of such large datasets would be time-consuming and prone to bias. However, AI algorithms can efficiently process textual data, identify sentiment patterns, and extract meaningful insights within seconds or minutes. This empowers businesses to stay up-to-date with customer feedback and sentiment, allowing them to respond promptly and appropriately.

By monitoring sentiment analysis results, businesses can gain valuable insights into customer satisfaction levels and identify areas of improvement. Positive sentiments can highlight aspects of the business that are performing well and can be leveraged to build on brand strengths. On the other hand, negative sentiments can signal potential issues that need to be addressed promptly to prevent reputation damage.

Reputation management goes hand in hand with sentiment analysis. Once sentiment data is collected, businesses can take proactive steps to manage their reputation effectively. AI-driven tools can assist in tracking and managing online reviews, social media mentions, and customer feedback. This allows businesses to promptly address negative comments, resolve customer issues, and turn negative experiences into positive ones.

AI-powered reputation management tools can also provide businesses with actionable insights and recommendations for improving customer experience and brand perception. By analyzing sentiment trends and identifying patterns, businesses can make data-driven decisions to enhance their products, services, and overall customer experience.

It is worth noting that while AI-driven sentiment analysis is a powerful tool, human oversight and interpretation are still crucial. AI algorithms may not always accurately capture the nuances of language and context. Therefore, businesses should ensure that sentiment analysis results are reviewed by human experts to validate accuracy and provide additional insights.

In conclusion, AI-driven sentiment analysis and reputation management offer businesses valuable tools for understanding customer sentiment, maintaining a positive brand image, and enhancing overall customer experience. By leveraging advanced algorithms to analyze vast amounts of data, businesses can make data-driven decisions, address customer concerns proactively, and continuously improve their products and services. The combination of AI technology and human expertise allows businesses to effectively manage their reputation in the digital landscape and build long-lasting relationships with customers.

Handling Customer Inquiries And Complaints Effectively

No matter how exceptional your products or services may be, there will always be instances where customers encounter issues or have inquiries. How you handle these situations can make or break the customer experience. In this segment, we provide you with practical guidance on effectively handling customer inquiries and complaints.

By utilizing AI-powered tools, you can streamline and automate your customer support processes, ensuring timely and accurate resolutions. We delve into the best practices for setting up efficient systems that enable customers to reach out easily and receive prompt assistance. Furthermore, we discuss the importance of empathy and active listening when dealing with customer concerns, demonstrating how these human elements combined with AI-driven support can lead to enhanced customer satisfaction.

Throughout this section, we emphasize the significance of incorporating AI technologies into your customer engagement and support strategies. By embracing AI chatbots, sentiment analysis, and effective complaint management, you can create a seamless customer experience that fosters loyalty, generates positive word-of-mouth, and ultimately contributes to the success of your business.

In the realm of customer support, the way businesses handle customer inquiries and complaints plays a crucial role in shaping the overall customer experience. With the advancements in AI technology, businesses now have powerful tools at their disposal to handle these interactions with efficiency and effectiveness.

AI-powered systems can streamline and automate the process of handling customer inquiries, ensuring that each query is addressed promptly and accurately. These systems can analyze customer messages, emails, or social media posts and categorize them based on their nature, urgency, or complexity. By automatically routing inquiries to the appropriate departments or agents, businesses can minimize response time and avoid unnecessary delays.

One key advantage of AI-powered systems is their ability to provide consistent and accurate information. Through machine learning algorithms, these systems can be trained on vast amounts of data, including FAQs, product information, and support documents. As a result, when customers reach out with common questions or concerns, AI-powered systems can provide instant and accurate responses, eliminating the need for customers to wait for human agents to retrieve the information.

Furthermore, AI technology can assist in sentiment analysis, allowing businesses to understand the emotional state of the customer and tailor their responses accordingly. By analyzing the tone and language used in customer inquiries or complaints, AI systems can identify the sentiment behind the message, whether it's frustration, satisfaction, or confusion. This enables businesses to respond with empathy and address the emotional aspect of the customer's concern, ultimately leading to a more positive and satisfactory resolution.

In addition to handling inquiries, AI technology can also assist in effectively managing customer complaints. AI-powered systems can automatically detect and flag complaints based on predefined criteria, ensuring that no customer concern goes unnoticed. These systems can prioritize and escalate complaints to the appropriate channels, ensuring that urgent issues receive immediate attention and resolution.

AI can also facilitate the process of tracking and following up on customer complaints. By automating case management, businesses can ensure that each complaint is properly documented, assigned, and tracked throughout the resolution process. This allows for better accountability, visibility, and collaboration among support teams, resulting in improved efficiency and customer satisfaction.

However, it's important to note that while AI technology can automate and optimize certain aspects of customer support, the human touch remains crucial. Customers value personalized interactions and appreciate the empathy and understanding that only human agents can provide. Therefore, businesses should strive to strike a balance between AI automation and human intervention, ensuring that complex or sensitive cases are appropriately escalated to human agents who can provide the necessary expertise and emotional support.

In conclusion, handling customer inquiries and complaints effectively is a critical component of providing exceptional customer support. AI-powered systems offer businesses valuable tools to automate and optimize this process, allowing for prompt and accurate responses, sentiment analysis, and efficient complaint management. By leveraging AI technology alongside human expertise, businesses can deliver a seamless and satisfying customer experience, building trust, loyalty, and positive brand perception.

Remember, mastering customer engagement and support is a continuous journey, and AI tools are here to assist you every step of the way. So, let's dive into the world of AI-driven customer interaction and unlock the potential to exceed customer expectations like never before.

CHAPTER 6

Influencer Marketing and
Collaborations

Influencer Marketing has become a powerful strategy in the world of social media. Collaborating with influencers can significantly boost your brand's reach, credibility, and engagement. In this chapter, we will explore how AI tools can help you identify the right influencers, build authentic relationships with them, and measure the impact of your influencer campaigns.

Identifying Influencers With AI Tools

Finding the perfect influencers for your brand can be a daunting task. Thankfully, AI tools have made this process much more efficient and effective. These intelligent tools can analyze vast amounts of data, including social media profiles, audience demographics, engagement rates, and content performance, to identify the influencers that align with your brand's values and target audience.

AI-powered influencer identification tools use advanced algorithms to filter through the noise and provide you with a curated list of potential influencers. By leveraging AI, you can save countless hours of manual research and gain valuable insights into an influencer's online presence, content style, and audience engagement.

In today's digital landscape, identifying the right influencers for your brand can be a game-changer in reaching and engaging your target audience. Fortunately, advancements in AI technology have made the process of identifying influencers much more efficient and effective. In this chapter, we will explore how AI tools can help you discover the perfect influencers for your brand's goals and objectives.

AI-powered influencer identification tools leverage machine learning algorithms to analyze vast amounts of data from various social media platforms. These tools can sift through millions of profiles, posts, and engagements to identify individuals who have a significant impact on your target audience.

One of the key advantages of using AI tools for influencer identification is their ability to process large quantities of data quickly. Instead of manually combing through countless profiles, AI algorithms can analyze data points such as follower count, engagement rate, content relevance, and audience demographics to provide you with a curated list of potential influencers.

By utilizing AI, you can save valuable time and resources that would have otherwise been spent on manual research. AI tools streamline the process by filtering out irrelevant or low-quality influencers, allowing you to focus your efforts on those who are more likely to align with your brand's values and resonate with your target audience.

AI-powered influencer identification tools also provide valuable insights into an influencer's content style and engagement patterns. Through sentiment analysis and content analysis algorithms, these tools can assess the tone and sentiment of an influencer's posts, ensuring that their content aligns with your brand's messaging and values.

Furthermore, AI tools can help you identify influencers who have an authentic and engaged audience. By examining the quality of engagement, such as genuine comments and interactions, AI algorithms can differentiate between influencers with real influence and those who may have inflated follower numbers or engagement rates.

It's important to note that while AI tools can provide a solid foundation for influencer identification, human judgment and intuition still play a vital role. AI should be used as a complement to human analysis and decision-making, allowing marketers to make informed choices based on both quantitative and qualitative factors.

AI tools have revolutionized the process of identifying influencers for brand collaborations. With their ability to analyze large volumes of data quickly and accurately, AI-powered influencer identification tools help marketers find influencers who are a perfect fit for their brand's goals and target audience. By leveraging the power of AI, you can streamline your influencer marketing efforts, save time and resources, and ultimately enhance the effectiveness of your social media management strategy.

Building Authentic Relationships With Influencers

Once you've identified the influencers who resonate with your brand, it's crucial to build authentic and meaningful relationships with them. AI can play a significant role in streamlining and enhancing this process.

AI-powered relationship management tools can help you stay organized and track your interactions with influencers. From initial outreach to ongoing collaborations, these tools enable you to maintain a personalized approach by keeping records of past conversations, preferences, and collaborations.

Additionally, AI can assist in analyzing an influencer's content and interests, allowing you to tailor your communication and collaboration proposals to their specific preferences. By demonstrating a genuine interest in their work and aligning your brand's values with theirs, you can foster trust and build long-term partnerships.

Building authentic relationships with influencers is a crucial aspect of successful influencer marketing campaigns. When done right, these relationships can lead to long-term partnerships and generate genuine engagement with your target audience. In this chapter, we will explore how to foster authentic connections with influencers and establish mutually beneficial collaborations using AI tools.

Personalization and Tailored Outreach: AI tools can help you gather relevant information about influencers, such as their interests, values, and previous collaborations. This data allows you to craft personalized outreach messages that resonate with each influencer on an individual level. By demonstrating that you have taken the time to understand their content and align your brand's values with theirs, you increase the likelihood of building a genuine connection.

Social Listening and Engagement: AI-powered social listening tools can monitor influencers' online activities, including their posts, comments, and conversations. By keeping track of their content and engaging with it genuinely, you can establish a meaningful presence and demonstrate your interest in their work. Engaging with influencers' content not only helps build relationships but also increases the chances of them noticing and engaging with your brand.

Collaboration Opportunities: AI tools can analyze influencers' content and audience demographics to identify potential collaboration opportunities that align with your brand's goals. By leveraging AI-driven analytics, you can identify synergies between your brand and the influencer's niche. This enables you to propose collaboration ideas that are relevant and appealing to both parties, enhancing the chances of building an authentic partnership.

Relationship Management Platforms: AI-powered relationship management platforms provide a centralized space to track your interactions with influencers. These platforms can store important details, such as previous conversations, collaboration history, and preferences. By having this information readily available, you can maintain a personalized approach when reaching out to influencers and avoid repetitive or generic interactions.

Influencer Feedback and Co-creation: AI tools can assist in analyzing the performance and impact of influencer collaborations. By gathering data on metrics such as engagement rates, website traffic, and conversions, you can assess the success of the collaborations and make data-driven decisions for future partnerships. Additionally, AI-powered sentiment analysis can help gauge audience sentiment towards the influencer and the brand, ensuring that the collaboration aligns with your brand's image and values.

Long-term Relationship Cultivation: Building authentic relationships with influencers requires a long-term perspective. AI tools can help you nurture these relationships by providing timely reminders for follow-ups, identifying opportunities for continued collaborations, and tracking influencers' career advancements. By staying updated on their journey and supporting their growth, you can build trust and foster long-lasting partnerships.

AI tools offer valuable assistance in building authentic relationships with influencers. By leveraging personalization, social listening, collaboration opportunities, relationship management platforms, influencer feedback, and long-term relationship cultivation, you can establish meaningful connections that go beyond transactional partnerships. Remember, while AI tools provide valuable insights, the human touch is essential for building genuine relationships. By combining the power of AI with thoughtful human engagement, you can create successful influencer collaborations that resonate with your audience and drive meaningful results for your brand.

Measuring The Impact Of Influencer Campaigns

Measuring the impact of your influencer campaigns is crucial to understanding their effectiveness and optimizing your marketing strategies. AI-powered analytics tools provide powerful insights into the performance of your influencer collaborations.

These tools can track key metrics such as reach, engagement, website traffic, conversions, and even sentiment analysis. By harnessing the power of AI, you can delve deeper into the data and uncover valuable trends and patterns that help you evaluate the success of your campaigns.

AI algorithms can analyze vast amounts of data in real-time, allowing you to make data-driven decisions and iterate your influencer marketing strategies. Whether it's identifying which influencers drive the highest ROI or understanding the content types that resonate best with your audience, AI-powered analytics give you the actionable insights you need to refine your influencer collaborations.

Measuring the impact of influencer campaigns is vital to understanding their effectiveness and optimizing your marketing strategies. In this chapter, we will explore how AI tools can help you accurately measure and evaluate the impact of your influencer campaigns, allowing you to make data-driven decisions and drive better results.

Tracking Key Metrics: AI-powered analytics tools enable you to track essential metrics that provide insights into the performance of your influencer campaigns. These tools can monitor metrics such as reach, engagement, website traffic, conversions, and even sentiment analysis. By tracking these metrics, you can assess the effectiveness of your campaigns and understand the level of audience engagement and interest generated by your influencer collaborations.

Advanced Data Analysis: AI algorithms excel in analyzing vast amounts of data quickly and accurately. By leveraging AI-powered analytics, you can gain deeper insights into the performance of your influencer campaigns. These algorithms can identify patterns, trends, and correlations within the data, helping you understand which influencers, content types, or collaboration strategies drive the most significant impact for your brand.

Attribution Modeling: AI tools can assist in attributing conversions or other desired actions to specific influencer campaigns. Through advanced attribution modeling, AI algorithms can analyze multiple touchpoints along the customer journey and determine the contribution of influencer collaborations to conversions. This helps you understand the direct impact of influencer marketing on your bottom line and optimize your budget allocation accordingly.

Real-time Monitoring: AI-powered tools provide real-time monitoring capabilities, allowing you to track the performance of your influencer campaigns as they unfold. This instant access to data enables you to make timely adjustments or optimizations to maximize the impact of your campaigns. Whether it's identifying underperforming influencers or adjusting content strategies based on audience feedback, real-time monitoring empowers you to be agile and responsive.

Sentiment Analysis: AI-driven sentiment analysis tools can assess the sentiment and public perception surrounding your influencer campaigns. By analyzing social media conversations, comments, and user-generated content, these tools can gauge the overall sentiment towards your brand and influencer collaborations. This information helps you understand how your campaigns are resonating with your audience and make informed decisions to address any issues or capitalize on positive sentiment.

Comparative Analysis: AI tools enable comparative analysis of different influencer campaigns or strategies. By comparing the performance of various influencers or content approaches, you can identify best practices and optimize future campaigns. AI algorithms can identify trends and patterns, allowing you to refine your targeting, messaging, or collaboration strategies for maximum impact.

Reporting and Visualization: AI-powered analytics tools often provide user-friendly dashboards and visualizations that make it easier to interpret and communicate campaign results. These reports offer clear insights into the performance metrics, trends, and key takeaways from your influencer campaigns. Visualizing the data through graphs, charts, or heatmaps helps stakeholders understand the impact of influencer marketing in a concise and digestible manner.

AI tools play a crucial role in measuring the impact of influencer campaigns. By tracking key metrics, utilizing advanced data analysis, implementing attribution modeling, real-time monitoring, sentiment analysis, comparative analysis, and generating comprehensive reports, AI empowers marketers to make data-driven decisions and optimize their influencer marketing strategies. By harnessing the power of AI, you can gain valuable insights, refine your campaigns, and achieve better results through influencer collaborations.

Conclusion:

Influencer marketing, when done right, can be a game-changer for your social media management strategy. By harnessing the power of AI tools, you can effectively identify influencers, build authentic relationships, and measure the impact of your influencer campaigns. Embrace the capabilities of AI, and unlock the full potential of influencer marketing to propel your brand's success in the dynamic world of social media.

CHAPTER 7

Staying Ahead of Social Media
Trends

AI-Powered Trend Analysis And Forecasting

In today's fast-paced digital landscape, staying on top of social media trends is crucial for businesses and content creators. Fortunately, the integration of AI-powered tools has revolutionized trend analysis and forecasting, empowering individuals and organizations to make informed decisions and stay ahead of the curve.

In this chapter, we will explore how AI can supercharge your trend analysis efforts. By harnessing the power of machine learning algorithms, AI tools can analyze vast amounts of data from social media platforms, identify patterns, and extract valuable insights. These insights enable you to understand what's resonating with your target audience, predict emerging trends, and tailor your content strategy accordingly.

In the rapidly evolving landscape of social media, keeping up with the latest trends is crucial for businesses and content creators. Thankfully, the integration of AI-powered tools has revolutionized trend analysis and forecasting, empowering individuals and organizations to make data-driven decisions and stay ahead of the competition.

AI, or artificial intelligence, has the capability to analyze massive amounts of data from various social media platforms. By employing advanced machine learning algorithms, AI tools can identify patterns, extract meaningful insights, and predict future trends. This enables businesses to understand what resonates with their target audience and tailor their content strategies accordingly.

One of the key advantages of AI-powered trend analysis is its ability to process data in real-time. Traditional methods of trend analysis often require manual data collection and analysis, which can be time-consuming and inefficient. AI tools, on the other hand, can continuously monitor social media platforms, collect relevant data, and provide up-to-date insights. This allows businesses to quickly adapt to emerging trends and capitalize on timely opportunities.

Moreover, AI-powered trend analysis can uncover hidden patterns and correlations within the data that may not be apparent to human analysts. By examining vast amounts of information, AI algorithms can identify relationships between different variables and provide a holistic view of trends. This deeper understanding enables businesses to make more accurate predictions and informed decisions.

AI-powered trend analysis also offers the advantage of scalability. As the volume of data generated by social media platforms continues to grow exponentially, it becomes increasingly challenging for human analysts to keep up. AI tools, however, are designed to handle large datasets and can process information at a much faster rate. This scalability ensures that businesses can effectively analyze trends even as data volumes increase.

To leverage AI-powered trend analysis effectively, businesses need to select the right tools and platforms that align with their specific needs. There are numerous AI-powered analytics platforms available, each offering unique features and functionalities. It's essential to evaluate these options and choose the tool that best suits your goals and requirements.

Furthermore, while AI can provide valuable insights, human judgment and creativity remain essential in interpreting and applying these findings. AI tools should be viewed as a complement to human expertise rather than a replacement. Combining the power of AI with human insights can lead to more comprehensive and effective trend analysis.

In conclusion, AI-powered trend analysis and forecasting have become indispensable tools for mastering social media management. By harnessing the power of AI, businesses and content creators can uncover valuable insights, predict emerging trends, and stay ahead of the competition. However, it's important to remember that AI tools should be used in conjunction with human expertise to maximize their potential. With the right combination of AI and human insights, businesses can navigate the ever-changing social media landscape with confidence and success.

Anticipating And Adapting To Industry Shifts

In the ever-evolving realm of social media, industry shifts and changes are inevitable. To thrive in this dynamic landscape, it's essential to anticipate these shifts and adapt your strategies proactively. With the help of AI, you can gain a competitive edge by closely monitoring industry trends and adjusting your approach accordingly.

This section will guide you through the process of anticipating and adapting to industry shifts. By leveraging AI tools, you can track industry developments, analyze competitor strategies, and identify emerging opportunities. With this knowledge, you can pivot your content creation and management efforts effectively, ensuring that your brand remains relevant and resonates with your audience.

In the dynamic world of social media, industry shifts and changes are inevitable. To thrive in this rapidly evolving landscape, businesses and content creators must be proactive in anticipating these shifts and adapting their strategies accordingly. By staying ahead of industry trends, they can seize opportunities, maintain relevance, and effectively engage their target audience.

Anticipating industry shifts involves keeping a close eye on emerging trends and changes within the social media landscape. It requires a combination of market research, competitor analysis, and staying informed about the latest developments. AI-powered tools play a crucial role in this process, as they can help businesses monitor industry trends, analyze competitor strategies, and identify emerging opportunities.

With the help of AI, businesses can gather and process vast amounts of data from social media platforms, news sources, and industry reports. These AI-powered analytics tools can identify patterns, detect shifts in consumer behavior, and provide valuable insights into the changing dynamics of the industry. By leveraging these insights, businesses can proactively adjust their content creation and management strategies to stay ahead of the curve.

Adapting to industry shifts requires agility and the ability to respond quickly to changing market conditions. It involves aligning content strategies with emerging trends and adjusting approaches to meet evolving consumer expectations. AI can facilitate this process by providing real-time data and actionable insights that guide decision-making.

For example, if an AI-powered analysis reveals a growing preference for video content among the target audience, businesses can adapt their content creation efforts to prioritize video production. They can invest in video editing tools, collaborate with videographers, or explore new video formats that resonate with their followers. By adapting to this industry shift, businesses can maintain a competitive edge and effectively engage their audience.

Another important aspect of adapting to industry shifts is monitoring and analyzing the performance of content. AI-powered analytics tools can track key metrics such as engagement rates, click-through rates, and conversion rates. By regularly monitoring these metrics, businesses can identify which content strategies are effective and which ones need adjustment. This iterative approach allows for continuous optimization and adaptation to industry shifts.

Additionally, businesses can leverage AI-powered social listening tools to gain insights into consumer sentiment and feedback. By monitoring social media conversations and brand mentions, businesses can identify emerging trends, address customer concerns, and adapt their strategies accordingly. This proactive approach not only helps businesses stay ahead of industry shifts but also strengthens their relationship with their target audience.

In conclusion, anticipating and adapting to industry shifts is essential for success in the ever-changing world of social media. AI-powered tools provide businesses with the ability to gather real-time data, identify trends, and make informed decisions. By staying proactive, monitoring industry shifts, and leveraging AI-driven insights, businesses can position themselves as industry leaders, maintain relevance, and effectively engage their audience in an ever-evolving social media landscape.

Incorporating Emerging Technologies In Social Media

As technology advances, new opportunities for innovation in social media arise. Incorporating emerging technologies into your social media management approach can elevate your content creation and engagement strategies to new heights. AI, augmented reality (AR), virtual reality (VR), and other cutting-edge technologies can enhance user experiences, boost brand engagement, and differentiate your content from competitors.

This chapter will explore how you can leverage emerging technologies in social media to captivate your audience. We will delve into the practical applications of AI, AR, VR, and other tools, providing real-world examples and best practices. By embracing these technologies, you can unlock exciting possibilities and create immersive experiences that leave a lasting impact on your followers.

By the end of this chapter, you will have a clear understanding of how AI-powered trend analysis, anticipating industry shifts, and incorporating emerging technologies can help you stay ahead of social media trends. Armed with this knowledge, you can adapt your strategies, deliver captivating content, and establish your brand as a frontrunner in the ever-evolving world of social media.

As technology continues to advance at a rapid pace, incorporating emerging technologies into social media strategies has become imperative for businesses and content creators. By embracing these cutting-edge tools, they can enhance user experiences, drive engagement, and gain a competitive edge in the ever-evolving landscape of social media.

One of the key emerging technologies that revolutionize social media is artificial intelligence (AI). AI-powered tools enable businesses to automate tasks, personalize content, and provide more interactive experiences. For instance, chatbots powered by AI can engage with users in real-time, answer frequently asked questions, and provide personalized recommendations. This not only improves customer satisfaction but also frees up human resources for more strategic initiatives.

Another emerging technology that is transforming social media is augmented reality (AR). AR overlays digital content onto the real world, enhancing users' perception and interaction with their surroundings. Businesses can leverage AR to create immersive experiences, such as virtual try-on features for fashion brands or interactive product demonstrations. By incorporating AR into their social media strategies, businesses can captivate their audience and provide memorable brand experiences.

Virtual reality (VR) is yet another technology with immense potential for social media. VR allows users to enter a simulated, three-dimensional environment, offering a truly immersive experience. Businesses can utilize

VR to showcase products, create virtual tours, or host virtual events, allowing users to engage with their brand in innovative ways. By leveraging VR, businesses can stand out from the competition and provide unique and captivating content to their audience.

In addition to AI, AR, and VR, there are other emerging technologies that businesses can incorporate into their social media strategies. For example, blockchain technology can enhance transparency and security in social media transactions, enabling more trusted interactions between businesses and consumers. Internet of Things (IoT) devices can provide real-time data streams that businesses can leverage to personalize content and deliver targeted messages. By embracing these technologies, businesses can tap into new opportunities and create differentiated experiences for their audience.

To effectively incorporate emerging technologies into social media strategies, businesses need to consider their target audience and the platforms they frequent. Each technology may have different applications and levels of adoption across various social media platforms. By understanding their audience's preferences and behaviors, businesses can tailor their use of emerging technologies to maximize impact.

It is worth noting that while emerging technologies offer tremendous opportunities, their implementation should be strategic and aligned with business objectives. It is essential to assess the feasibility, scalability, and potential impact of each technology before integration. A well-thought-out plan ensures that businesses can effectively utilize emerging technologies to enhance their social media presence and achieve their goals.

Incorporating emerging technologies in social media can provide businesses with a competitive advantage and elevate their engagement strategies. From AI to AR, VR, blockchain, and IoT, these technologies offer innovative ways to interact with the audience, personalize content, and create immersive experiences. By staying informed about emerging trends, understanding their audience, and strategically integrating these technologies, businesses can navigate the evolving social media landscape with confidence and deliver compelling experiences to their followers.

Remember, staying ahead of the curve requires constant learning and adaptation. So, let's dive in and explore the exciting possibilities that AI and emerging technologies bring to the realm of social media management.

CHAPTER 8

Ethics and Responsible AI Usage

In today's digital landscape, as AI becomes an integral part of social media management, it is crucial to consider the ethical implications and responsible use of these powerful technologies. In Chapter 9, "Ethics and Responsible AI Usage," we delve into key considerations for maintaining a socially conscious approach to AI implementation in content creation and social media management.

Ensuring Privacy And Data Protection

In the rapidly evolving landscape of social media management powered by AI, it is crucial to prioritize privacy and protect sensitive data. As businesses harness the potential of AI algorithms to optimize their content creation and management strategies, safeguarding user information becomes an ethical imperative.

In this chapter, we delve into the critical considerations and best practices for ensuring privacy and data protection in the realm of AI-driven social media management. We explore the measures that organizations must take to maintain the trust of their audience while reaping the benefits of AI technology.

Transparency and Consent:

The foundation of data privacy lies in transparency and informed consent. Ensure that your users are fully aware of the data you collect, how it will be used, and any third parties involved. Implement clear and concise privacy policies and terms of service that users can easily access and understand. Obtain explicit consent from users before collecting and processing their data, and provide them with the option to modify or withdraw consent at any time.

Secure Data Storage and Transmission:

Data breaches can have severe consequences for both businesses and users. Employ robust security measures to protect user data from unauthorized access, theft, or misuse. Utilize encryption protocols to secure data during transmission and storage. Regularly update security systems and promptly address any vulnerabilities that may arise.

Minimization of Data Collection:

Adopt a principle of data minimization, which means collecting only the data necessary for your social media management activities. Limiting the data you collect reduces the risk associated with storing and handling vast amounts of user information. Evaluate the purpose of each data point and collect only what is essential for providing personalized content and improving user experience.

Anonymization and Aggregation:

When possible, aggregate and anonymize user data to protect individual identities. By analyzing trends and patterns from aggregated data, you can glean valuable insights without compromising the privacy of individual users. Strive to strike a balance between data utility and anonymity.

Compliance with Data Regulations:

Stay updated with relevant data protection regulations, such as the General Data Protection Regulation (GDPR) in Europe or the California Consumer Privacy Act (CCPA) in the United States. Ensure that your social media management practices align with these laws and that you fulfill any legal obligations related to user data rights, such as data access and deletion requests.

Regular Data Audits and Assessments:

Conduct periodic data audits to evaluate the data you collect, process, and store. Assess the security measures in place and identify any potential risks to data privacy. These audits will help you maintain compliance, improve data protection, and build trust with your audience.

By prioritizing privacy and data protection in your AI-driven social media management strategies, you demonstrate respect for your users' rights and foster a sense of trust and loyalty. Upholding stringent data privacy practices not only protects your users but also safeguards your brand reputation in an increasingly data-conscious world.

Addressing Bias And Fairness In AI Algorithms

AI algorithms have the potential to revolutionize social media management, but they are not immune to biases that exist in the real world. In this chapter, we explore the importance of addressing bias and promoting fairness in AI algorithms used for content creation and management.

We delve into the various forms of bias that can emerge in AI algorithms and their potential impact on user experiences. Through thought-provoking examples and case studies, we highlight the significance of unbiased and fair AI systems in fostering inclusivity and avoiding discriminatory outcomes.

AI algorithms have transformed the way we interact with technology and make decisions, including those related to social media management and content creation. However, these algorithms are not infallible, and they can inadvertently perpetuate biases present in the data they are trained on. Addressing bias and ensuring fairness in AI algorithms is of utmost importance to maintain ethical and equitable practices in social media management.

Understanding Algorithmic Bias:

Algorithmic bias refers to the systematic errors or prejudices that AI algorithms can exhibit when making decisions or predictions. Bias can emerge from biased data, the design of the algorithm, or the context in which the algorithm is deployed. In social media management, biased algorithms can result in unequal representation, discrimination, or reinforcement of stereotypes in content creation and distribution.

Identifying Bias in AI Algorithms:

Recognizing and understanding bias in AI algorithms is the first step towards addressing it. This involves conducting thorough audits of the AI models and analyzing the data used for training. It's essential to consider various dimensions of bias, including racial, gender, socioeconomic, and cultural biases, among others, to ensure a comprehensive assessment.

Mitigating Bias during Training:

Developers and data scientists must take proactive measures to mitigate bias during the training phase. This includes carefully curating training data to ensure it is representative and diverse. Additionally, techniques such as data augmentation, reweighting, and adversarial training can be employed to reduce bias in AI algorithms.

Fairness-aware Algorithm Design:

Fairness-aware algorithm design focuses on developing AI models that explicitly take fairness into account. This means incorporating fairness constraints during the model development process to avoid producing discriminatory outcomes. Fairness-aware techniques strive to achieve equitable results across different demographic groups.

Regular Monitoring and Evaluation:

Bias in AI algorithms can change over time as social contexts evolve, new data is incorporated, or the algorithm itself is updated. Thus, continuous monitoring and evaluation are crucial to ensure that AI systems remain fair and unbiased in their decision-making processes.

Inclusivity and Diverse Stakeholder Involvement:

Building fair AI algorithms requires diverse perspectives and expertise. Involving individuals from different backgrounds and communities in the design, development, and evaluation of AI systems can help identify potential biases and ensure a more inclusive approach to social media management.

Transparency and Accountability:

Transparency about AI usage and decision-making processes is essential to maintain trust with users and stakeholders. Social media managers should be transparent about the role of AI in content creation and sharing and be open about their efforts to address bias and ensure fairness.

By actively addressing bias and fairness in AI algorithms, social media managers can create a more inclusive and equitable online environment for their audience. Embracing responsible AI practices not only enhances brand reputation but also contributes to a positive and diverse digital space for everyone.

Furthermore, we present actionable strategies to identify and mitigate bias in AI algorithms. By adopting these techniques, you will be equipped to create and manage content that resonates with diverse audiences, ensuring inclusivity and fairness across your social media platforms.

Balancing Automation And Human Touch

While AI technology empowers us to automate numerous aspects of social media management, it is essential to strike a balance between automation and the human touch. In this chapter, we explore the delicate equilibrium required to create compelling and authentic content while leveraging the advantages of AI-driven automation.

We delve into the role of human creativity and intuition in content creation, emphasizing the irreplaceable value of human insights and emotions. By understanding how to harness the power of AI tools while preserving the human element, you will be able to create engaging content that connects with your audience on a deeper level.

In the realm of social media management with AI, finding the delicate equilibrium between automation and the human touch is essential to achieve optimal results and maintain a genuine connection with your audience. Chapter 9 explores the significance of this balance and provides practical insights on how to strike the right chord between leveraging AI's efficiency and preserving the authenticity of human interaction.

Leveraging AI Automation:

AI-powered automation tools offer unparalleled efficiency and scalability in managing social media content, scheduling posts, analyzing data, and even responding to customer inquiries through chatbots. In this section, we delve into the benefits of using AI for automation, saving time and resources while streamlining various aspects of social media management.

Enhancing Consistency and Speed:

Automation ensures that your content is consistently delivered to your audience at optimal times, allowing you to maintain a steady online presence and engage with followers across different time zones. We explore how AI can help you respond swiftly to trends and developments, ensuring your brand remains relevant and responsive in the fast-paced world of social media.

Preserving the Human Touch:

While automation is powerful, we recognize the irreplaceable value of human creativity and empathy. This part discusses the importance of crafting content that resonates emotionally with your audience, nurturing meaningful connections, and building a strong sense of community. We explore how to infuse human insights into AI-generated content to maintain an authentic and relatable voice.

Engaging with Genuine Interactions:

AI can handle routine customer queries and support, but it is vital to recognize the instances when a human touch is indispensable. We explore the art of personalized customer engagement, demonstrating how genuine interactions can foster trust, loyalty, and positive brand sentiment.

Monitoring and Quality Control:

While AI can automate various tasks, human oversight is crucial to maintain quality and ensure that the AI algorithms align with your brand's values. We discuss strategies for monitoring AI-generated content and intervening when necessary to prevent potential miscommunications or unintended consequences.

Feedback and Continuous Improvement:

The synergy between AI and the human touch can be enhanced through continuous feedback loops. We explore the importance of gathering insights from your audience and your team to refine AI algorithms, enhance personalization, and strengthen customer relationships.

Striking the right balance between AI automation and the human touch is an ongoing process of learning, adjusting, and refining. In Chapter 9, we equip you with the knowledge and strategies to create an AI-driven social media management approach that maximizes efficiency while maintaining a strong and authentic connection with your audience. By embracing the strengths of both automation and human creativity, you can elevate your social media presence to new heights while keeping your brand's identity and values at the forefront.

Navigating the ethical landscape of AI in social media management is not only a responsibility but an opportunity to build a more sustainable and trustworthy online presence. In Chapter 9, we equip you with the knowledge and tools to make informed decisions, foster transparency, and use AI in a manner that aligns with your brand values and respects the rights and interests of your audience.

CHAPTER 9

Future of Social Media Management with AI

I n this captivating chapter, we dive headfirst into the exciting realm of the future of social media management with AI. Prepare to be amazed as we explore the ever-evolving landscape of AI technologies and their applications in the realm of social media.

Evolving AI Technologies and Applications: Discover the cutting-edge advancements that are revolutionizing the way we manage social media. From sophisticated machine learning algorithms to natural language processing, we uncover the tools that will shape the future of content creation and management.

The world of social media management is experiencing a profound transformation. This chapter delves into the groundbreaking advancements that are reshaping the way we approach content creation and management.

Discover the power of sophisticated machine learning algorithms that can analyze vast amounts of data, allowing you to extract valuable insights and make data-driven decisions. Unleash the potential of natural language processing, enabling you to automate content generation, sentiment analysis, and even personalized customer interactions.

Witness the emergence of computer vision, empowering you to create visually stunning and engaging content with the help of AI-powered image and video analysis. Explore the possibilities of voice recognition and natural language understanding, revolutionizing the way users interact with social media platforms.

As AI technologies continue to evolve, exciting new applications are being unlocked. From chatbots that provide instant customer support to recommendation systems that curate personalized content, the potential for AI-driven social media management is boundless.

However, along with these incredible opportunities come challenges that must be navigated. Ethical considerations surrounding data privacy, algorithmic bias, and the responsible use of AI must be carefully addressed. Striking the right balance between automation and the human touch remains an ongoing challenge.

By embracing these evolving AI technologies and understanding their applications, you can harness their power to elevate your social media management to new heights. Prepare to embark on a journey that will reshape your approach to content creation, engagement, and customer satisfaction.

In the next section, we will explore the predictions and trends that will shape the future of social media management with AI, allowing you to stay ahead of the curve and position yourself as a leader in this dynamic field.

Predictions and Trends for the Future: Gain exclusive insights into the trends and predictions that will shape the social media landscape in the coming years. Stay ahead of the curve as we forecast the emerging technologies, strategies, and consumer behaviors that will impact your social media management journey.

As we gaze into the future of social media management with AI, we uncover a world of exciting predictions and emerging trends that will shape the landscape. By staying informed and adaptable, you can position yourself at the forefront of this rapidly evolving field. Here are some key predictions and trends to watch out for:

Hyper-Personalization: AI will enable social media managers to deliver highly personalized experiences to users. Advanced algorithms will analyze user behavior, preferences, and demographics to tailor content and recommendations, fostering deeper engagement and stronger connections.

Augmented Reality (AR) Integration: AR will become increasingly integrated into social media platforms, offering immersive and interactive experiences for users. From virtual try-on experiences to AR filters and effects, brands will leverage AI-powered AR tools to captivate and engage their audiences.

Voice and Visual Search: Voice and visual search capabilities will continue to grow in popularity. AI-powered voice assistants and visual recognition technologies will enable users to search for content, products, and services simply by speaking or capturing images, transforming the way users discover and engage with social media content.

Influencer Identification and Verification: AI algorithms will play a crucial role in identifying and verifying influencers. Advanced tools will analyze follower engagement, content quality, and authenticity to help brands and marketers identify the most relevant and trustworthy influencers for collaborations and partnerships.

Automated Content Curation: AI-powered content curation will become more refined and efficient. Algorithms will analyze user interests, preferences, and engagement patterns to curate personalized content feeds, saving time and effort for social media managers while enhancing user experiences.

Enhanced Customer Service with AI Chatbots: AI chatbots will continue to improve and offer more sophisticated customer service experiences. Natural language processing and machine learning will enable chatbots to understand

and respond to customer inquiries with greater accuracy and empathy, providing efficient support around the clock.

Ethical AI and Transparency: As AI becomes more prevalent in social media management, the need for ethical considerations and transparency will grow. Stricter regulations and guidelines will emerge to ensure fair and responsible AI usage, addressing concerns related to data privacy, bias, and algorithmic transparency.

By keeping a pulse on these predictions and trends, you can adapt your social media management strategies and leverage AI tools to stay ahead of the competition. The next section will explore the opportunities and challenges that lie ahead, helping you navigate this exciting future with confidence.

Opportunities and Challenges Ahead: With every new frontier comes a set of opportunities and challenges. Explore the vast potential that AI offers for optimizing your social media presence, while also addressing the ethical considerations and potential pitfalls that come with leveraging this powerful technology.

As we gaze into the future of social media management with AI, we uncover a world of exciting predictions and emerging trends that will shape the landscape. By staying informed and adaptable, you can position yourself at the forefront of this rapidly evolving field. Here are some key predictions and trends to watch out for:

Hyper-Personalization: AI will enable social media managers to deliver highly personalized experiences to users. Advanced algorithms will analyze user behavior, preferences, and demographics to tailor content and recommendations, fostering deeper engagement and stronger connections.

Augmented Reality (AR) Integration: AR will become increasingly integrated into social media platforms, offering immersive and interactive experiences for users. From virtual try-on experiences to AR filters and effects, brands will leverage AI-powered AR tools to captivate and engage their audiences.

Voice and Visual Search: Voice and visual search capabilities will continue to grow in popularity. AI-powered voice assistants and visual recognition technologies will enable users to search for content, products, and services simply by speaking or capturing images, transforming the way users discover and engage with social media content.

Influencer Identification and Verification: AI algorithms will play a crucial role in identifying and verifying influencers. Advanced tools will analyze follower engagement, content quality, and authenticity to help brands and marketers identify the most relevant and trustworthy influencers for collaborations and partnerships.

Automated Content Curation: AI-powered content curation will become more refined and efficient. Algorithms will analyze user interests, preferences, and engagement patterns to curate personalized content feeds, saving time and effort for social media managers while enhancing user experiences.

Enhanced Customer Service with AI Chatbots: AI chatbots will continue to improve and offer more sophisticated customer service experiences. Natural language processing and machine learning will enable chatbots to understand and respond to customer inquiries with greater accuracy and empathy, providing efficient support around the clock.

Ethical AI and Transparency: As AI becomes more prevalent in social media management, the need for ethical considerations and transparency will grow. Stricter regulations and guidelines will emerge to ensure fair and responsible AI usage, addressing concerns related to data privacy, bias, and algorithmic transparency.

By keeping a pulse on these predictions and trends, you can adapt your social media management strategies and leverage AI tools to stay ahead of the competition. The next section will explore the opportunities and challenges that lie ahead, helping you navigate this exciting future with confidence.

In this illuminating chapter, we empower you to embrace the future with confidence, equipping you with the knowledge and foresight needed to navigate the ever-changing world of social media management with AI. Get ready to unlock a world of possibilities and seize the opportunities that lie ahead.

CONCLUSION

In this journey through the realm of social media management enhanced by AI, we have uncovered a wealth of knowledge and practical strategies for content creation. As we come to the end of our exploration, let us take a moment to recap the key learnings we have acquired and reflect on the transformative power of AI in shaping the social media landscape.

Throughout this handbook, we have delved into the benefits of leveraging AI in social media management, from streamlining content creation processes to optimizing audience engagement. We have witnessed how AI-powered tools can inspire and assist in crafting captivating headlines, captions, and visuals, breathing life into your brand's online presence.

By automating content scheduling and posting, we discovered how AI can free up valuable time and resources, enabling you to focus on strategic initiatives. Additionally, we explored the importance of analyzing performance metrics and using AI analytics tools to uncover insights that drive results and refine our social media strategies.

In our quest to master social media management, we also recognized the power of AI in managing customer engagement and support. With the assistance of AI chatbots and sentiment analysis, we can deliver personalized experiences, address inquiries efficiently, and protect our brand's reputation.

We ventured into the world of influencer marketing, learning how AI tools help identify and build authentic collaborations. By measuring the impact of influencer campaigns, we gain a deeper understanding of their effectiveness and make data-driven decisions to maximize our return on investment.

As we examined the ever-evolving social media landscape, we explored AI-powered trend analysis and forecasting. This foresight allows us to stay one step ahead, adapt to emerging industry shifts, and embrace new technologies that push the boundaries of social media management.

Throughout our journey, we also touched upon the ethical considerations and responsible usage of AI. By ensuring privacy, addressing bias, and finding the delicate balance between automation and the human touch, we can create a social media ecosystem that is both efficient and morally grounded.

Now, armed with these key learnings, it is time to take action. The path to mastering social media management with AI lies in applying the knowledge gained and implementing actionable steps. Whether it's refining your content creation process, fine-tuning your posting schedule, or deepening customer engagement, let these insights be the catalyst for transformative change.

Remember, the future of social media management is constantly evolving, and embracing AI will undoubtedly be a crucial aspect of staying ahead. As you navigate this dynamic landscape, continue to seek out new knowledge, stay informed about emerging technologies, and adapt your strategies to meet the ever-changing needs of your audience.

With the power of AI at your fingertips and the wisdom gained from this practical handbook, you are now equipped to master the art of social media management. Unleash your creativity, seize opportunities, and build meaningful connections that propel your brand to new heights.

Congratulations on completing this journey. Your mastery of social media management with AI awaits.

Appendix

In this appendix, you'll find valuable resources to enhance your understanding and proficiency in mastering social media management with AI. We've carefully curated a glossary of key terms, ensuring that you have a comprehensive grasp of the terminology used in the field.

Additionally, we provide a list of recommended AI tools and resources that will empower you to take your content creation skills to new heights. These tools have been handpicked to support your journey in leveraging AI's potential for social media management, enabling you to streamline your processes and achieve remarkable results.

Furthermore, we understand the importance of staying informed and up-to-date in this rapidly evolving field. That's why we've included a meticulously curated selection of references and further reading materials. These resources will serve as your compass, guiding you to the latest insights, trends, and best practices in social media management with AI.

By delving into the glossary, exploring the recommended AI tools, and diving into the suggested references, you'llRemember, in this digital age, staying ahead requires continuous learning and adaptation. Embrace the power of AI, and let this practical handbook be your trusted companion as you embark on your journey to mastering social media management. equip yourself with the knowledge and tools necessary to navigate the dynamic landscape of social media management with confidence and finesse.

Glossary of Key terms

Artificial Intelligence (AI): A branch of computer science that focuses on creating intelligent machines capable of performing tasks that would typically require human intelligence.

Content Creation: The process of developing and producing valuable and engaging materials, such as articles, videos, images, or infographics, for distribution on social media platforms.

Social Media Management: The practice of planning, organizing, and executing social media strategies to establish and maintain a strong online presence, engage with the target audience, and achieve marketing goals.

Algorithm: A set of rules or instructions followed by a computer program to solve a problem or perform a specific task. In social media management, algorithms are used to determine content visibility, relevance, and user experience.

Analytics: The collection, measurement, analysis, and interpretation of data to gain insights into social media performance, audience behavior, and engagement metrics.

Chatbots: AI-powered virtual assistants designed to interact with users in a conversational manner, providing automated customer support, answering inquiries, and assisting with various tasks on social media platforms.

Influencer Marketing: A marketing strategy that involves collaborating with influential individuals (influencers) on social media to promote products, services, or brands and leverage their influence to reach a wider audience.

Sentiment Analysis: The process of using AI algorithms to identify and analyze the sentiment (positive, negative, or neutral) expressed in social media posts, comments, or reviews.

Automation: The use of technology, such as AI tools, to streamline and optimize repetitive tasks in social media management, saving time and increasing efficiency.

Trend Analysis: The examination of patterns, changes, and emerging topics or behaviors on social media platforms to identify trends that can inform content creation and strategy development.

Privacy and Data Protection: The measures and regulations in place to ensure the confidentiality, integrity, and security of personal and user data collected and processed in social media management.

Bias: Systematic deviations or preferences in AI algorithms that may result in unfair or discriminatory outcomes. Addressing bias in AI is crucial to ensure ethical and equitable social media management practices.

ABOUT THE AUTHOR

Temitope Aluko

 Temitope Aluko, a marketing and communications manager with over a decade of experience in digital marketing. With expertise in digital strategy, online marketing, lead generation, retargeting, PPC advertising, and social media marketing, Temitope Aluko has helped numerous clients and brands achieve their marketing goals through effective online strategies.

As a skilled web developer using PHP and WordPress, Temitope Aluko creates and maintains engaging websites that drive traffic and conversions. In addition, Temitope Aluko's passion for creative content writing and keen eye for detail allows them to develop engaging content that resonates with audiences and drives conversions.

Temitope Aluko specializes in B2B solutions, with a focus on helping companies in the software-as-a-service and legal industries with their lead generation and user acquisition efforts. Their full-funnel activation approach, combined with expertise in keyword research and lead scoring, ensures that clients' campaigns are effective and results-driven.